M000247916

# design
## furniture

Editorial Director
Nacho Asensio

Coordinating and editing
Patricia Bueno

Design
Núria Sordé Orpinell

Translation
Mark Parent

Production
Juanjo Rodríguez Novel

Copyright © 2003 Atrium Group
Proyecto editorial: Books Factory, S.L.
e-mail: books@booksfactory.org

Published by: Atrium Group de ediciones y publicaciones, S.L.
c/ Ganduxer, 112
08022 BARCELONA

Telf: +34 932 540 099
Fax: +34 932 118 139
e-mail: atrium@atriumgroup.org
www.atriumbooks.com

ISBN: 84-95692-93-7
Legal registration:

Printed in Spain
ANMAN Gràfiques del Vallès, S.L.

All rights reserved. The reproduction, whole or in part, of this work in any form or by any means, including reprography or data processing treatments,
and the distribution of copies either for hire or public lending, are strictly prohibited without the written authorisation of the copyright holders, and subject to the penalties prescribed by law.

# INDEX

# INTRODUCTION

At a popular level, it is common to associate the concept of "design furniture" with uncomfortable, impersonal objects, that generate cold atmospheres and are the result of capricious fashions and therefore are destined to wear out quickly and become quickly obsolete. True design, however, goes far beyond this definition. In the first place, because good designs are destined to remain permanent in time, to become eternal, and resist the changes of fashion and tendencies. This is the case of the furniture that we present in the **Historical Introduction**, a symbol of modernity and 50 to 75 years after its conception, it will continue to be in style.

In the second place because, in spite of the undeniable importance that aesthetics has always had, well-designed furniture, by definition, fulfills a function beyond the its formal aspect, as it contributes to improve the quality of life of its users.

But..., what is it that converts a piece of furniture into something memorable? There are numerous factors and disciplines that the designer and the company must bear in mind on defining the concept of the product so that it brings together exceptional qualities: *anthropology* in respect to the study of man in society which allows us to understand his motivations and needs and respond to or anticipate them; *ergonomics*, which makes objects adapt to the physical characteristics of people, improving their comfort and facilitating their use; *technical innovation*, by means of research into and the application of new technologies, materials and means of production; *sustainability* and *ecology*, in respect to the development of articles that are compatible with the natural resources to be found in the surrounding environment; the consideration of the social, ethical, moral and environmental questions that confer *meaning* to the resulting product whether it be an ashtray, a tap or a sofa; *critical thinking* since the most relevant contemporary designers are characterized by their constant questioning of prevailing norms and preestablished concepts regarding furniture; apart from equally important aspects such as economy, art, engineering, etc.

The interrelation of all these factors allows a concept of industrial design to take place, within which we find the design of furniture, quite different from what we saw at the beginning. Thus, in the strictest and most professional sense of the term, design becomes a complex expression of the aesthetic, social, economic, political and technological forces of a society, besides being a powerful tool in business strategy and management, increasing the productivity of those companies in the sector that use industrial design as a fundamental element in their reason for being.

In definitive, we could conclude that design in order to be qualified as "good", must be able to maintain the balance between art and technology, between spontaneity and research, between shape and function, between aesthetics and ergonomics, between innovation and tradition, between matter and spirit, or, to say it in another way, between body and soul.

This criteria was taken as a point of reference on deciding the selection of all the articles that this book illustrates. All types of examples of articles which could be included in our domestic environment are included, signed by the most creative minds of the moment and produced by companies which have adopted good design as their distinctive feature. The objective is that these pieces will be able to go beyond current fashion and that they will be equally attractive 100 years from now as they are today. Notwithstanding, of course, time will have the final say about this.

# HISTORICAL INTRODUCTION

"Everlasting modernity is the measure
of merit of any piece of art"
Ralph Waldo Emerson (1803-1882),
North American poet,
philosopher and essayist.

The history of design in the twentieth century is the shared passion of men and women with an innovative spirit, whose desire was to improve the society that they lived in. In order to do this they researched, developed and applied new materials and production methods in the manufacture of furniture and household articles, thus achieving that quality and well-designed furniture were available to the majority of the population and not only to, as it had happened up to then, a select minority. From this perspective then design acquires intellectual and philosophical connotations, as it questions the way of life of society of the moment, thus providing formal, functional and technical solutions. In each decade the historical, political, sociological and cultural context influenced the general lines of design significantly. One of the most illustrative examples was the growth in industrialization which the two world wars provided which offered technological innovations that afforded new aesthetic opportunities.

Perhaps the changes with the greatest historical repercussions were those that occurred up until the decade of the sixties. The aesthetic and conceptual movements which make up the foundation of contemporary design occurred in those years. That time provided us with furniture that is considered works of art, and it is even put on exhibition in the best museums of the world, where retrospective exhibitions of the greatest designers of the world are held. The majority of the designers, and not by chance, were also great architects, and their names are written in the history of the twentieth century.

From the beginning of the century creators such as, Michael Thonet, William Morris, Antonio Gaudí, Frank Lloyd Wright, Charles Rennie Mackintosh, Joseph Hoffmann, Eileen Gray, Mies van der Rohe, Le Corbusier, Walter Gropius, Gerrit Thomas Rietveld, Alvar

Sofa designed by Marcel Breuer
in 1931. *Tecta*.

Armchair "LC1" by Le Corbusier,
P. Jeanneret and C. Perriand,
1928. *Cassina*.

"Barcelona" chair,
by Mies van der Rohe, 1929.
(photo: *Vitra* Museum).

Chair "611" designed in 1926 by
Alvar Aalto. *Artek*.

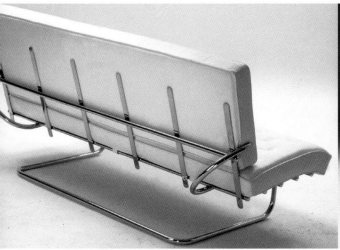

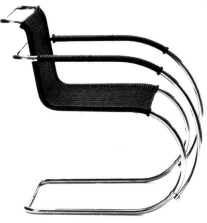

"Plastic Chair" by Charles &
Ray Eames, 1948. *Vitra*
(photo Hans Hansen)

"Follia" by G. Terragni,
1934. *Zanotta*.

"Cone Chair" and "Cone Table" by Verner Panton, 1958.
*Vitra*. (photo Hans Hansen)

Design by Mies van der Rohe,
1927. *Tecta*.

Design by Walter Gropius,
1920. *Tecta*.

Chair designed by Michael Thonet in 1859.
*Thonet*.

7

Design by Jean Prouvé.
*Tecta.*

Aalto, Jean Prouvé, Marcel Breuer, Arne Jacobsen, Charles & Ray Eames, Verner Panton, Eero Aarnio o Ettore Sottsass, among many others, have provided us with technical and aesthetic innovations that have contributed to improve our quality of life, and have shaped the appearance of our present household environment.

On some occasions the articles created are attributed to one of the artistic movements that have occurred throughout the century, whereas on other occasions it is difficult to label them with the name of one specific movement. Regarding their influence in the contemporary design of furniture and household articles, these are the most important movements that have taken place in the century:

**-1900-1910:** In Europe the century began under the influence of two movements, **arts & crafts** and **art nouveau**. The first arose in England around 1860, as a reform movement led by John Ruskin and William Morris. They defended a return to the handcraft methods of the Middle Ages, as a reaction against the dehumanization imposed by society due to the growing industrialization and mass production. Their objective was to create furniture with a design based on natural materials, simple and honest forms, handcraft and utility. On the other hand, art nouveau arose at the end of the nineteenth century and it replaced historical styles that were predominate at the time.

The style was characterized by sensual designs based on organic shapes inspired from nature, and reflecting a strong influence from Japanese art. Among its exponents we include Victor Horta, Louis Comfort Tiffany and René Lalique. The style found in Viena a version with more rectilinear shapes, which put a special emphasis on functionality, with designers like Adolf Loos and Josef Hoffman, who found a source of inspiration in the designs of the Scotsman Charles Rennie Mackintosh with his contribution of geometric lines.

**-1910-1920:** Two important aesthetical and ideological movements, De Stijl and the Bauhaus School, appeared on the scene in these years. The **De Stijl** Group developed between 1917 and 1928 with representatives of the category of Piet Mondrian, in painting, and Gerrit Rietveld the creator of some of

"Panton Chair" by Verner Panton, 1967/69. *Vitra* (photo H. Hansen).     "Wire Chair" by Charles & Ray Eames, 1951. *Vitra* (photo H. Hansen).

"La Chaise" by Charles & Ray Eames, 1948. *Vitra* (photo H. Hansen).

"Anthony" by Jean Prouvé, 1950. *Vitra.*

"Plywood Chair" by Charles & Ray Eames, 1946. *Vitra.*

"Lounge Chair" by Charles & Ray Eames, 1956. *Vitra* (photo H. Hansen).

"Sella" by A. and P.G. Castiglioni, 1957. *Zanotta*

Armchair designed by Alison and Peter Smithson. *Tecta.*

"Maggiolina" by M. Zanuso, 1947. *Zanotta.*

the most well-known furniture of twentieth century design. The aesthetics of the group were based on the explicit use of primary colors and in the exploration of shape which implied a certain dosis of minimalism, both formal and spiritual. In respect to the **Bauhaus** School which was functioning from 1919 till 1933, the importance that it exerted on design and architecture in the twentieth century, is undeniable. One of the principal tenets of the School, established by the founder, Walter Gropius, was to attain that "…. modern artists become familiar with science and economy, bringing together creative imagination and a practical sense of handcrafting, and consequently developing a new sense of functional design". They were attempting, therefore, the integration of all the disciplines of art, design, handcrafting and architecture in order to produce a completely designed and unified environment. With the firm conviction that economical and practical objects should also be beautiful, the **Bauhaus** designer promoted the use of industrial materials and explored the problem of mass production to furnish the homes of the middle class. Thus, they tried to link the gap between social idealism and commercial reality, promoting a reply to the emerging technological culture. Their components defended the virtues of **functionalism**, which asserted that the shape of an object was determined by its function and the materials used. Marcel Breuer, with innovative designs based on his experiments with tubular steel, or Mies van der Rohe, with designs of refined lines also based on the technical possibilities of steel, are two of the maximum representatives of Bauhaus in respect to furniture design.

At the same time, at the end of the twenties, Le Corbusier y Charlotte Perriand experimented in France with the possibilities that aluminum had to offer, which led to some of the most emblematic furniture of the twentieth century.

-**1920-1940:** In this period between the two wars an eclectic style known as **art deco** was developed. It refers to this art and also both architecture and the design of interiors. The name is an abreviation of the *Exposition Internationale des Arts Décoratifs et Industriels Modernes*, which took place in Paris in 1925, where the style was exhibited for the first

"Bubble Chair" by Eero Aarnio, 1968. *Adelta.*

"Cité Chair" by Jean Prouvé, 1931. *Vitra* (photo H. Hansen).

"Ball Chair" by Eero Aarnio, 1962. *Adelta.*

"Lamp" by Gerrit Rietveld, 1920. *Tecta.*

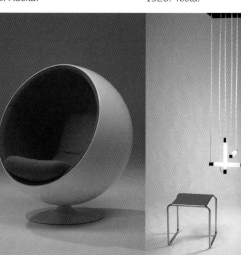

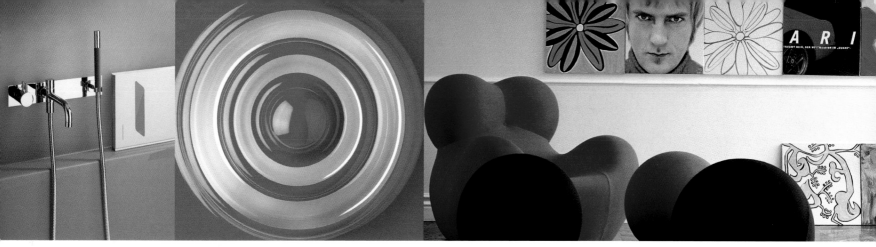

Faucets designed by
Arne Jacobsen, 1968. Vola.

"Ring Lamp" by Verner Panton.
*Vitra.* (photo A. Sütterlin)

"Serie Up" by Gaetano Pesce,
1969. *B & B Italy.*

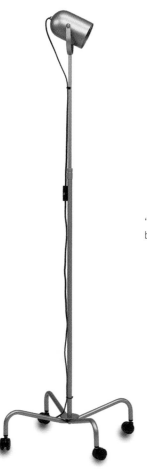

"Panto Beam Lamp"
by Verner Panton. *Innovation.*

Chair design by Marcel Breuer,
1926. *Tecta.*

Design by Mies van der Rohe, 1932. *Tecta*.

time as a celebration of life in the modern world. The reflection of a period of great contradictions from the happy-go-lucky roaring twenties to the Great Depression of the thirties, the architecture and the applied arts of this period reflect a great variety of influences: art nouveau, the Bauhaus style, cubism and Russian Ballet are among the influences that shaped it.

In respect to decorative aspects, inspiration was taken from the culture of American Indians, Egypt, and from classical shapes and from nature. In spite of the variety of sources, the designs of this period share certain distinctive points: geometry and simplicity, often combined with bright colors and new materials, led to simple shapes full of elegance which exalted the rise of commerce and technology. Among its favorite motifs, female nudes, animals, leaves of trees and rays of sunlight, stand out particularly. Thus under the Art Deco denomination we can find objects ranging from luxury objects made from exotic materials to industrially manufactured articles accessible to the emerging middle class. In both cases there is a shared attempt to create a pure line and anti-traditional elegance which symbolizes richness and sophistication. The interiors of the Rockefeller Center, the Chrysler Building or the Empire State Building are some of the most monumental examples of art deco.

On the other hand, in the middle of the thirties a new way to understand the creation of furniture emerged which was known as **Scandinavian organic design**. In contrast to the severity and utilitarianism of design inspired from the theories of Bauhaus, Scandinavian designers proposed a greater emphasis on natural materials and organic shapes. In this way the geometric lines and hard contours gave way to softer and more irregular biomorphic shapes in Denmark, Sweden and Finland. Instead of steel and glass, plywood, generally a light color, was used as a raw material which provided suggestive shapes that adapted better to the human body. Among its greatest exponents we can find the Finnish designer Alvar Aalto and the Danish architect and designer Arne Jacobsen whose importance has last to the present days. Following in the footsteps of these

Designs by Jean Prouvé: "Standard Chair", 1934; "Trapeze Table", 1950-54; "Potence Lamp", 1950. *Vitra*.

"Wassily Chair" by Marcel Breuer, 1925. Knoll, *Thonet*. (photo Glas).

"Moragas Lamp" by A. de Moragas, 1957. *Santa & Cole* (photo Carmen Masiá).

"LC2" by Le Corbusier, P. Jeanneret and C. Perriand, 1929. *Cassina*.

"Tac" inspired from an original design by Walter Gropius. *Rosenthal.*

"Moon Lamp" by Verner Panton. *Vitra* (photo A. Sütterlin)

"Gatpac" by Josep Torres Clavé, 1934. *Santa & Cole* (photo Carmen Masiá).

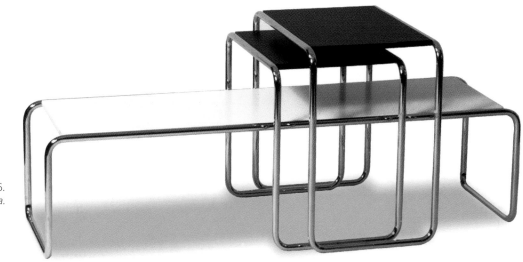

Tables designed by Marcel Breuer, 1926. *Tecta.*

designers, the couple Charles and Ray Eames developed experiments in the United States to mold plywood which gave rise to ergonomically designed chairs and armchairs which are still in style today in all the world.

**-1950-60:** A new aesthetic renovation took place led by the **pop art** movement which proved to be an injection of life for applied arts, as it reflected freshness and irony of popular culture by means of an intense range of colors and the utilization of new materials especially plastic. Consequently, pop design represented a challenge to the notions of tradi-

tion and longevity, giving rise to amusing and throw-away furniture whose design was based on the pictures in comics. This type of furniture which explored vulgarity, courseness and bright colors, made from synthetic, low-cost, throw-away materials, became the symbol of economic growth in the sixties. Parallelly, the arrival of man on the moon generated a futuristic type style inspired from the space race at the end of the sixties. The use of plastic allowed designers greater liberty to create all types of shapes and to use all types of colors which gave rise to furniture which combined fun with functionality. Among the pioneers who used this new material in industrial design was the Dane, Verner Panton one of the great names in pop aesthetics who developed the first inflatable furniture and the first projecting chair made entirely from

one piece of plastic (the so-called Panton Chair); the Finnish Eero Aarnio with his famous ball-shape or bubble-shape seats; or the Italian Joseph Colombo one of the most influential Italian designers who put special emphasis on the experimentation with new types of plastic and new types of technology, in an attempt to create the domestic environment of the future.

**-1970-1980:** In the middle of the seventies, **postmodernism** emerged as a confrontation to the principles of the modern movement whose aesthetics had dominated architecture and design for most of the twentieth century. In contrast to the austerity, rigidness and homogeneity of functionalism, young designers introduced irrational, sensual, humorous, colorful and surprising elements in order to recuperate the spontaneity, the complexity and

"Breuer Sofa" by Marcel Breuer, 1936. *Isokon Plus.*

"Crutches Lamp" by Salvador Dalí, 1937. *Bd Ediciones de Diseño.*

"Cadaqués Sofa" by F. Correa and A. Milá, 1959. *Santa & Cole* (photo Carmen Masiá)

"Long Chair" by Marcel Breuer, 1936.
*Isokon Plus.*

"66 Chair" by Alvar Aalto, 1933. *Artek.*

"Musser Table" by Frank Lloyd Wright, 1899.
*Cassina* ("Cassina I Maestri" Collection).

"Saturn" inspired from a design by Josef Albers, 1926. *Tecta.*

the capacity to surprise, thus creating interiors which were a stimulus to the imagination. In Italy various design groups, or anti-design groups with a revolutionary spirit, emerged whose ideas were a mixture of philosophy, art and industrial production. They used ornamentation which was almost considered taboo at the time, in order to provoke new meanings in the objects that they produced, thus clashing with the imposed notion of "good taste". Among these groups the collective known as **Memphis** stands out which was founded by Et-

tore Sottsass with the collaboration of young creators such as A. Branzi, Michele de Lucchi or Aldo Cibic. Their first exhibition in 1981 caused a great clamor and attracted designers from all over the world like Javier Mariscal, Robert Venturini, Masanori Umeda, Arata Isozaki, Matteo Thun, Richard Sapper, Carlos Riart, Hans Hollein, Shiro Kuramata, etc. Using elements from pop art, classicism, art deco, and in general anything which appeared attractive to the designer, Memphis style exerted a great influence on design and placed Italy in the center of the postmodernism movement. This style is characterized by the use of bright colors, the introduction of entertaining elements, intense contrasts, a free experimentation with materials, processes, shapes, textures and

drawings, the introduction of laminated, stamped surfaces, the creation of shapes that defy logic, and in definitive, designs where meaning predominates over the shape and the function, which is a reflection of contemporary culture.

Within postmodernism the role of **historicism** stands out which asserts that the past is as important as the present, thus combining classic styles with contemporary concepts, which generates a kind of stylistic anarchy. Among the most significant representatives we can find Léon Krier and Michael Graves.

Among the present great designers that began their career following the wake of postmodernism, we can find Phillippe Starck, Marc Newson, Jasper Morrison, Mario Botta or Ron Arad.

"TMM" by Miguel Milá, 1961. *Santa & Cole.* (photo Carmen Masiá).

"Leda Armchair" by Salvador Dalí, 1935. *Bd Ediciones de Diseño.*

"Zig-Zag" by Gerrit T. Rietveld, 1934. Cassina ("Cassina I Maestri" Collection).

"Bar Stool Nº 2" by Eileen Gray. *Classicon.*

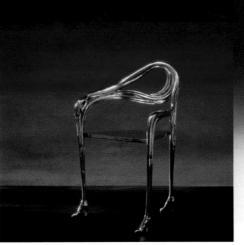

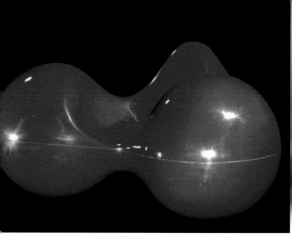

"Tomato Chair" by Eero Aarnio,
1971. *Adelta.*

"Daisies" Collection by Andy Warhol.
*Rosenthal.*

"Portrait" Collection by Andy
Warhol. *Rosenthal.*

"Lipari" Table by
Ettore Sottsass. *Zanotta.*

"Breuer-Thonet" Chair
designed in 1929/1930 by
Marcel Breuer. *Thonet.*

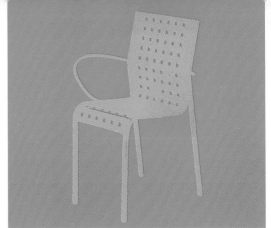

# LOUNGES AND DINING ROOMS

Perhaps it is in these environments where industrial designers have a greater margin for innovation. Sofas, bookcases or wood construction, armchairs, coffee tables or dining room tables, buffets, chairs or lamps, are elements that allow for experimentation with new shapes and materials, and offer innumerable possibilities for creativity.

For example, chairs, in spite of being one of the most basic pieces of furniture that exist, they have experienced a constant evolution since the beginning of the twentieth century when they were all manufactured according to the traditional shape. In the words of the designer George Nelson, "every truly original idea, each innovation in design, each new application of materials, each new technical development applied to the manufacture of furniture, seems to find its most important expression in a chair".

But in order that the furniture that makes up our living rooms and dining rooms becomes something that is really memorable and long-lasting in time, the designer must bear in mind some fundamental aspects: functionality, since each of these objects must fulfill the objective for which they were created; ergonomy, which will allow them to adapt to the anatomy of the people, affording comfort as well as utility; understanding and responding to the real needs of the users, and improving their quality of life; the reflection of new social tendencies, such as the need to save space, or the flexibility of pieces of furniture; the application of new materials and technologies that improve the quality of the finished product or reduce its cost, etc. The union of these factors, together with attractive shapes and materials, will permit the differentiation of the product based on its excellence.

"Rooby" Armchair by *Leolux*.

"Morgana" Bench with drawers by *Lago*.

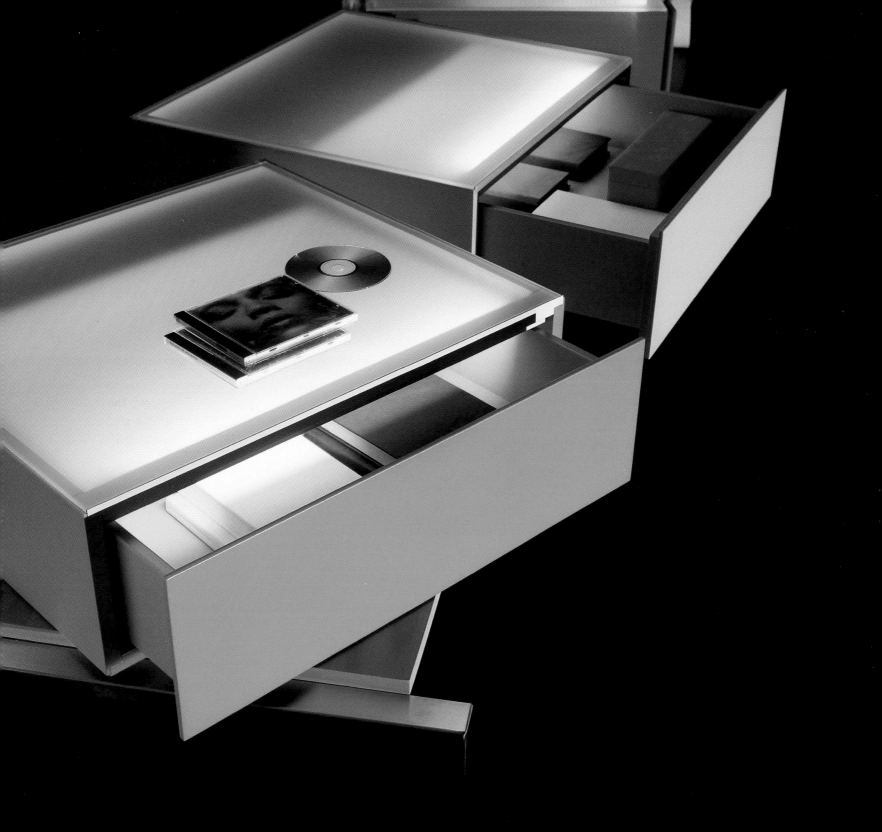

"900" Armchair.
*Fredericia Furniture.*

"Rooby" Sofa. *Leolux.*

"VK Chaise" by Vladimir Kagan.
*Kagan New York Collection.*

"Serpentine" Sofa by Vladimir Kagan.
*Kagan New York Collection.*

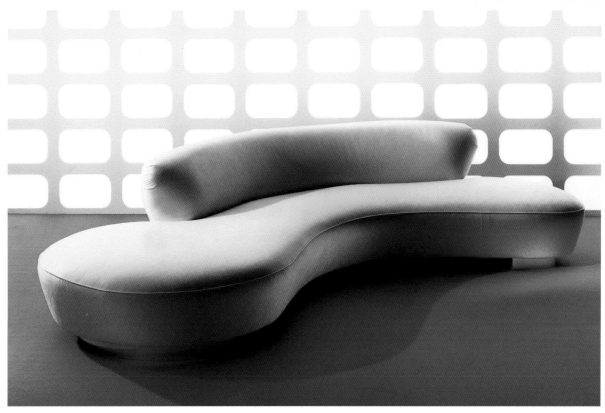

"Scroll" Seat set by Studio Vertijet.
*Cor.*

"Circolo" Rug by Bettina Hermann.
*Rolf Benz.*

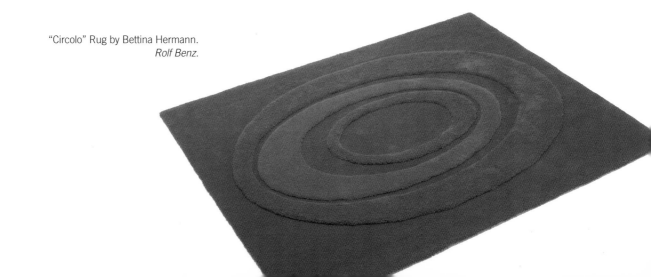

"Nemo" Sofa by Peter Maly. *Cor.*

"Delfina" Chair by Enzo Mari. *Robots.*

"Magazine" by Heitlinger Design. *Calligaris.*

"Kira" Armchair by
J. Brönte. *Bonaldo.*

"Olo" Sofa by Simone Micheli. *Adrenalina.*

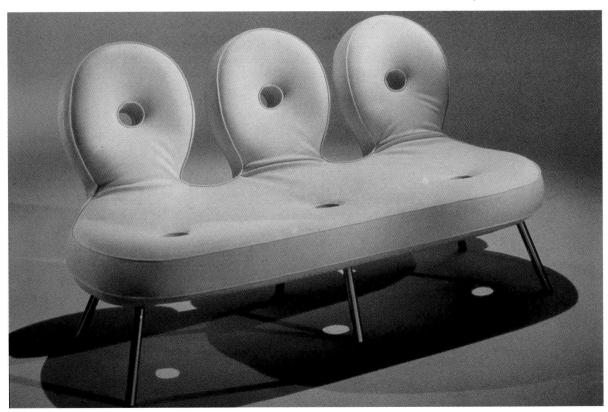

"Ampolla" Chair. *Lago.*

"Icon" Armchair by Nanna Ditzel.
*Fredericia Furniture.*

"Peel" Armchair by Olav EldØy. *Stokke.*

"Vermelha" Chair by Fernando and Humberto Campana. *Edra.*

"Joggle" Container System by Design for Use and Sergio Suchomel. *Magis.*

"Globulo" Inflatable Armchairs by
F. Bertero and A. Panto. *Zanotta.*

"Molly" Armchair by F. Bertero
and A. Panto. *Zanotta.*

"Plus Unit" Container System by
Werner Aisslinger. *Magis.*

"New Secret" Shelves Program by Pierangelo Galloti and Ricardo Bello Dias. *Gallotti & Radice.*

"Rem" Lamp by David Abad. *Dab.*

"Alhambra" Lamp with polypropylene diffuser by Ray Power. *Luzifer.*

"Monopoli" Chaise Longues by S. Giobbi and A. Mazonni Delle Stelle. *Busnelli.*

Multiple Combination Container System. *Maisa.*

"Pop" Rug by Pablo Gironés.
*Gandía Blasco.*

Container System. *Maisa.*

Composition of the "Niki" Program
by Ennio Arosio. *Mobileffe.*

"Wibber" Armchairs. *Leolux.*

"Nemo" Armchair by Peter Maly. *Cor.*

Sofa from the "Blox" Series
by Piero Lissoni. *Matteograssi.*

Rocking Chair with a
wooden back. *Vibiemme.*

"Onda" Chaise Longue by Jonas Kressel
and Ivo Schelle. *Cor.*

"Openside" Seat System by
Franco Poli. *Matteograssi.*

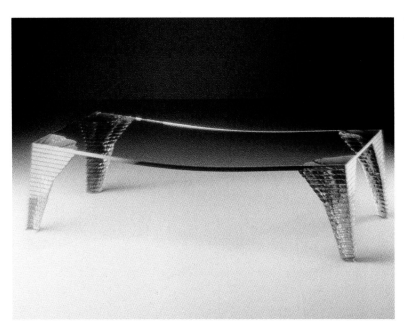

"Atlas" Coffee Table by Philippe Starck.
*Fiam Italy.*

"Nomada" Shelves by Giuseppe Canavese.
*Methodo.*

"Lucellino Wall" Lamp designed
and produced by *Ingo Maurer*.

Composition of the "Hey-Gi" System.
*Misura Emme.*

Rugs from the "Dots" Collection designed and produced by *Nani Marquina.*

Rug from the "Dots" Collection by *Nani Marquina.*

"Trama" Rug from the Sybila Collection.
*Nani Marquina.*

"Box" Buffet by Cà Nova Design.
*Cattelan Italy.*

"Big Air" Chair with a footrest.
*Calligaris.*

"Lultimo" Vase by L'Anverre.
*Zanotta.*

"Astrolenny" Candleholder by L'Anverre.
*Zanotta.*

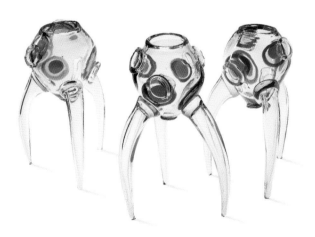

"In & Out" Jugs by L'Anverre. *Zanotta.*

"Unit" Cocktail Table by Gianni Astolfi and Sergio M. Mian. *Calligaris.*

"Sui" Lamp by Carlotta de Bevilacqua. *Artemide.*

"Apta" Armchair by
Antonio Citterio. *Maxalto.*

"Yoohoodoo" Suspension Lamp designed
and produced by *Ingo Maurer.*

"Radar" Armchair.
*B & B Italy.*

"Saga" Armchair by Gioia
Meller Marcovicz. *Classicon.*

"Press" Magazine Rack
by Enzo Mari. Robots.

"Mariposa" Chair by R. Dalisi.
*Zanotta.*

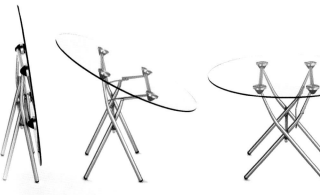

"Tomo" Fold-up Dining Room
Table. *Yamakado.*

Wood Construction from the
"Quadratus" Program. *Tisettanta.*

"The Globe" Cd Holder from the Living
Design Collection. *Miscel·lània.*

"Gem" Sofa with methacrylate sides by
Lodovico Acerbis. *Acerbis International.*

"Ferro" Dining Room Table
by Piero Lissoni. *Porro.*

"Flap" Sofa with reclining back
by Francesco Binfaré. Edra.

44

"Jetsons" Armchairs by Guglielmo Berchicci.
*Giovannetti.*

Sofa from the "Double" series
by Piero Lissoni. *Matteograssi.*

"Eleven" Dining Room Table with adjustable height. *Calligaris.*

"Poker" Game Table by J. Colombo. *Zanotta.*

"Ypsilon" Dining Room Set by Gijs Papavoine. *Montis.*

"Funnel" Floor Lamp by Ramón Benedito. *Vibia.*

"Spot" Bench.
*Mobili by Fredericia.*

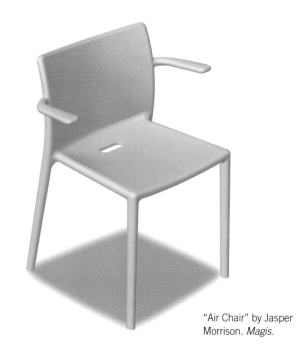

"Air Chair" by Jasper
Morrison. *Magis.*

"Helical Basic" Armchair. *Leolux.*

"Naked" Chair by Giovanni
Tommaso Garattoni. *Tonelli.*

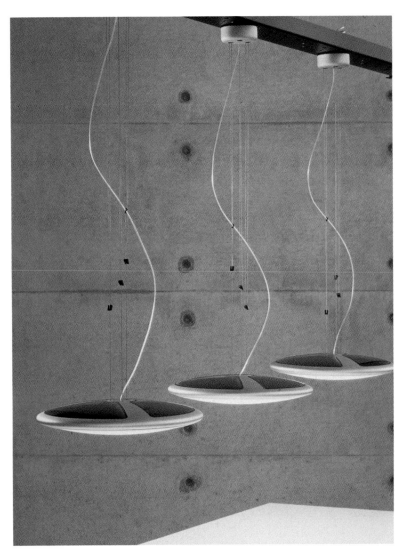

"Project X" Suspension Lamp
by *Tobias Grau*.

"Ala" Floor Lamp with a gray,
felt shade. *Diemo Alfons*.

"Frame" Television and Video Table from the Living Design Collection. *Miscel·lània.*

"Astra" Reclining Armchair. *Bodema.*

"Roly Poly" Armchair by Guido Rosati. Manufacture in more than 300 colors. *Giovannetti.*

"Net" Holder System. *Lago.*

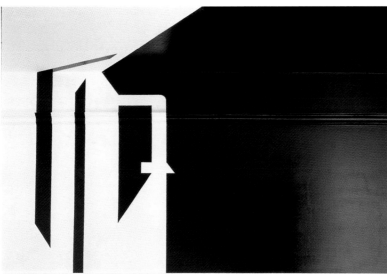

"Tulip" Armchair by Jeffrey Bernett.
*B & B Italy.*

«Kokoro» Lamp,
from The MaMo Nouchies collection by *Ingo Maurer*.

"Tom Vae" Chair
by Ron Arad. *Vitra.*

"Marina" by Enzo Mari.
*Zanotta.*

"Love" Armchairs by F. Scansetti
and M. Paul. *Insa.*

"2300" Sofa by Christian Werner.
*Rolf Benz.*

"Malabar" Seat Set. *Yamakado.*

Holder Type Furniture from the "Intu"
Program by Niels Bendtsen. *Montis.*

"Marocco" Sofa, "Stripe" Chest of Drawers and
"Asmir" Table by Paola Navone. *Casamilano.*

"Madison" Buffet from Cà Nova Design.
*Cattelan Italy.*

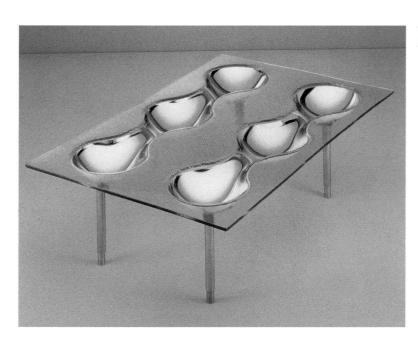

"Konx" Coffee Table by Ron Arad.
*Fiam Italy.*

"D.F. Uno" Armchair by Diego Fortunato.
*Perobell.*

"Alfa" Sofa by Emaf Progetti. *Zanotta.*

"Malou" Seat Set by Gijs
Papavoine. *Montis.*

"Greg" Chaise Longue by Emaf Progetti. *Zanotta*.

"Dandy" Seat Set by Gijs
Papavoine. *Montis*.

"Chaos" Armchair by Konstantin Grcic.
*Classicon*.

"Scultura" Seat with central light by Simone Micheli. *Adrenalina.*

"Zettel'z" Suspension Lamp designed and produced by *Ingo Maurer.*

58

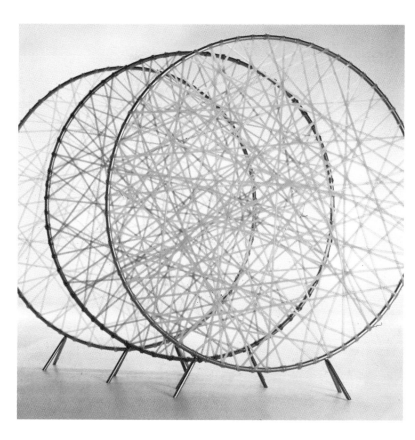

"Zig Zag" Screens by Humberto and Fernando Campana. *Edra*.

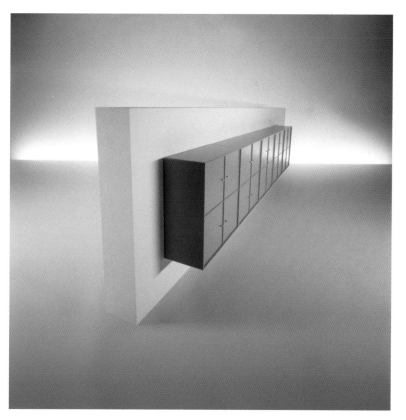

Modular Holder-type Furniture. *Montana*.

«Poul Poul» Lamp from the MaMo
Nouchies collection by *Ingo Maurer*.

"Bicho" Lamp Set by Pascal Frot for the
Luzitroniks Collection. *Luzifer.*

"Oh Mei Ma Kabir" Suspension Lamp
by *Ingo Maurer.*

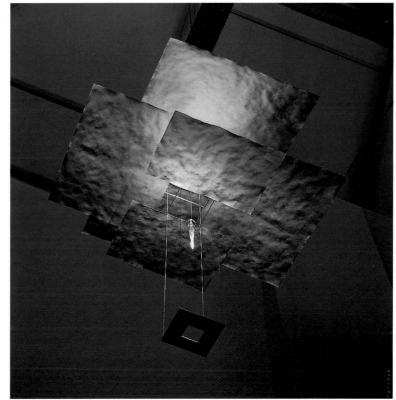

"Hara" by Carlotta de Bevilacqua. *Artemide.*

"Dida" Dining Room Table.
*Rafemar.*

"Eleonoire" Chair by Cà Nova Design.
*Cattelan Italy.*

"Karui" Magazine Rack. *Viccarbe.*

"Alhambra" Lamp in the floor lamp
version by Ray Power. Luzifer.

"Circo" Dining Room Table by Peter Maly. *Cor.*

"Aida" Chair by Richard Sapper. *Magis.*

"April" Chair with a leather back. *Matteograssi.*

"Big Bombo" Table
by Stefano Giovannoni. *Magis.*

"Bombo" Chair by Stefano Giovanoni. *Magis.*

"Tip Toe" in the floor version by Ramón Isern. *Vibia.*

"Poppea" Chair by Enrico Tonucci. *Triangolo*.

"Anemone" Seat by Humberto and Fernando Campana. *Edra*.

"Taber" Table and "Tiber" Buffet by Lievore, Altherr and Molina. *Muebles DO+CE.*

Chairs from the "Programa 890" by Lievore, Altherr and Molina. *Thonet.*

"Mirandolina" by P. Arosio.
*Zanotta.*

"Hula Hoop"
by Philippe Starck. *Vitra.*

"Globus" by Jesús Gasca. *Stua.*

"Halo" by Karim Rashid. *Magis.*

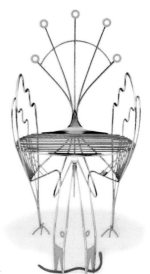

"Pavone" by R. Dalisi. *Zanotta.*

"Butterfly" by Karim Rashid. *Magis.*

"Hans" by Philipp Mainzer. *e15.*

"V2" Dining Room Table by Kasper Salto.
*Fredericia Furniture.*

"Max" Dining Room Table by
Gabrielle and Oscar Buratti.
*Acerbis International.*

"Milano" Dining Room Set.
*Lambert.*

"Cone" by Humberto and
Fernando Campana. *Edra.*

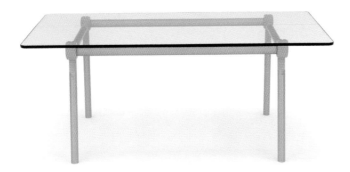

"Techno Table" by Christophe Pillet.
*Magis.*

"Reale" by C. Mollino.
*Zanotta.*

"Azimut" by Gijs Papavoine. *Montis.*

"Sanmarco" Table by G. Aulenti.
*Zanotta.*

"Omega" Table by Gijs Papavoine.
*Montis.*

"You" Dining Room Table.
*Calligaris.*

"Azul" Chair by Fernando and
Humberto Campana. *Edra.*

"Piuma" Chair by Studio Kronos.
*Cattelan Italy.*

"Spiral" Cocktail Table by Cà Nova Design.
*Cattelan Italy.*

"Delta" System Shelves
by Enzo Mari. *Robots.*

75

"Equis" Buffet by Jorge Pensi.
*Muebles Do+Ce.*

Buffet from the "Do it" Program.
*Viccarbe.*

"Airone" Sofa by S. Giobbi and
A. Mazzoni delle Stelle. *Busnelli.*

Buffet from the "Apta" Program
by Antonio Citterio. *Maxalto.*

"Bombo" Armchair with footrests
by Stefano Giovannoni. *Magis.*

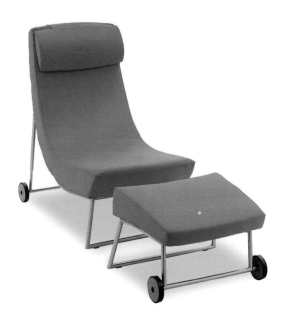

"Dream" by Heitlinger Design. *Calligaris.*

"Pororoca" by Flavia Alves de Souza.
*Edra.*

"Laguna" by Enzo Mari.
*Triangolo.*

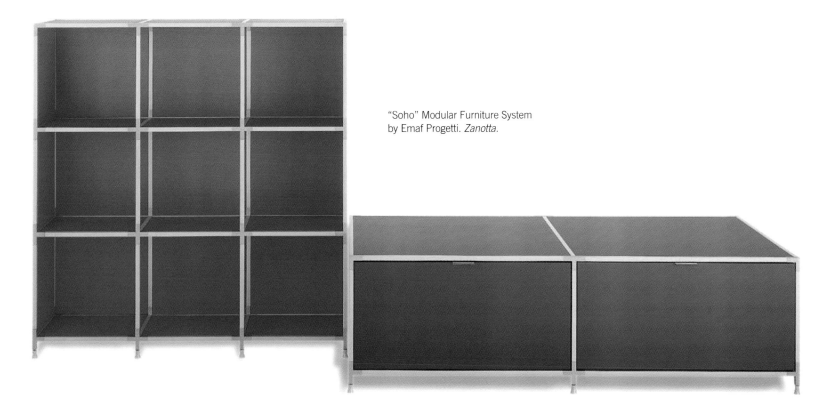

"Soho" Modular Furniture System
by Emaf Progetti. *Zanotta.*

79

"Oh China" Suspension Lamp with a china porcelain diffuser. *Tobias Grau.*

"Olvidada" Floor Lamp by Pepe Cortés.
*Bd Ediciones de Diseño..*

"Huevo de Colón" Floor Lamp by G. Ordeig.
*Santa & Cole* (photo Carmen Masiá).

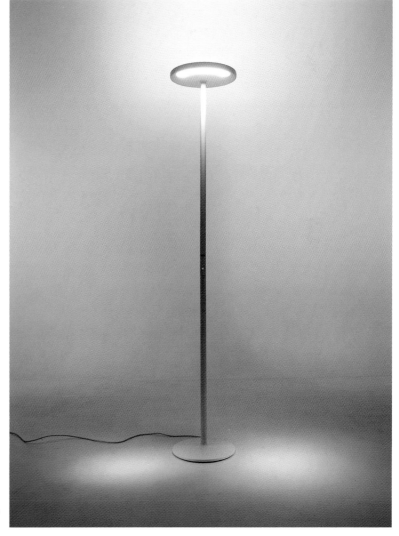

"One-Two" Floor Lamp
by James Irvine. *Artemide.*

81

"Long Chair 2000" by Mauro Lipparini.
*Rolf Benz.*

"Circo" Chairs by Peter Maly. *Cor.*

"Onda" by De Pas, d'Urbino and Lomazzi.
*Zanotta.*

"Cirrus" by Peter Maly. *Cor.*

"Folio" by Alfred Kleene and
Gabrielle Assmann. *Zanotta.*

"Loop" by Lucci & Orlandini. *Calligaris.*

"Rooby" Coffee Table. *Leolux.*

"C & C Night" Auxiliary Table by Christophe Pillet.
*Fiam Italy.*

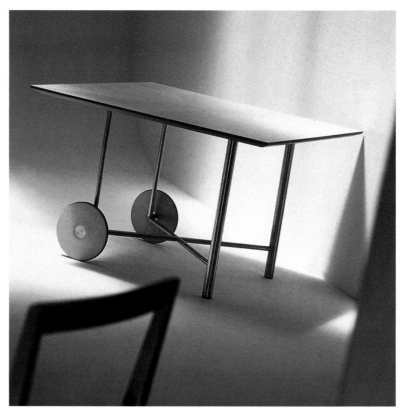

"Ojala" Dining Room Table by Carlos Riart. *Santa & Cole*
(photo Carmen Masiá).

"Estadio" Suspension Lamp by Miguel Milá.
*Santa & Cole* (photo Carmen Masiá).

Dining Room Set from the "Apta" Program
by Antonio Citterio. *Maxalto.*.

"Tube" by Bartoli Design.
*Rossi di Albizzate.*

"Supersassi" by Matteo Thun.
*Rossi di Albizzate.*

Armchair from the "Supersassi"
Collection by Matteo Thun. *Rossi di Albizzate.*

"Shu" Seat and Auxiliary Table Set by
Bartoli Design. *Rossi di Albizzate.*

"Acrobat" Armchair with an extendable
footrest by J. Armgardt. *Styling.*

"Moon" Armchair by Ferran Estela.
*Perobell.*

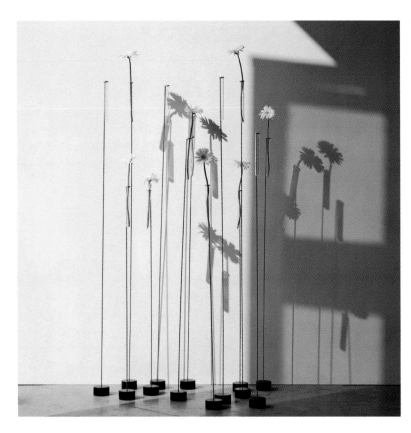

"Beta" Vases. *Rafemar.*

"Smilla" Chairs by Piergiorgio Cazzaniga.
*Acerbis International.*

"Ho" by Luca Meda.
*Molteni & C.*

"Meditation Pod" Seat
by Steven Blaess. *Edra.*

Buffet that combines wood,
glass and steel. *Club 8 Company.*

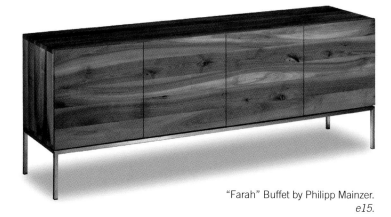

"Farah" Buffet by Philipp Mainzer.
*e15.*

"Le Pause" Chest of Drawers.
*Mobileffe.*

Holder Type Furniture from the "Intu"
Program by Niels Bendtsen. *Montis.*

Buffet on wheels from the "Street" Collection.
*Klenk Collection.*

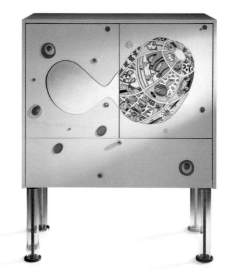

"Undercontrol" Buffet by E. de Paris.
*Zanotta.*

91

"Espa" Chairs by Ben af Schultén.
*Artek.*

Tables from the "Brighella" Series by
Lorenzo Arosio. *Glas.*

Composition from the "Silver"
Collection by Leoardo Volpi. *Edra.*

"Dry" extendable Dining Room Table
by Archivolto. *Bonaldo.*

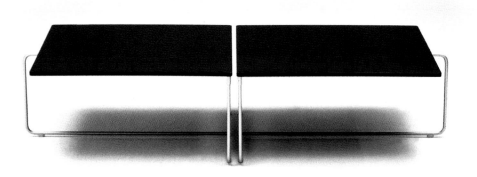

"Big Sister" Auxiliary Tables by
Lissoni Associati. *Artelano.*

"Elisa" leather upholstered Chair.
*Matteograssi.*

"Gas" Chair by Jesús Gasca.
*Stua.*

Tables from the "Romana" Series by Rafael Moneo.
*Bd Ediciones de Diseño.*

"Intu" Modular Furniture System
by Niels Bendtsen. *Montis.*

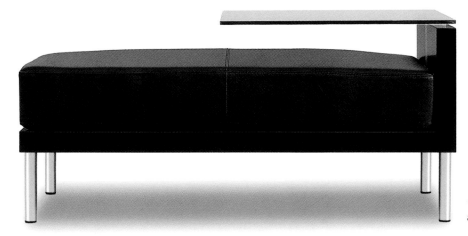

"Pavus" by Alfred Kleene
and Gabrielle Assmann. *Cor.*

"Porca Miseria" Suspension Lamp
by *Ingo Maurer*.

«Ierace» Suspension Lamp
by Matali Crasset. *Artemide*.

«In gamba» Coffee Table by
Julia Oozsa. *Tonelli*.

CD container «Helix», from Living
Design Collection. *Miscel·lània*.

# BEDROOMS

As in the other rooms of the house, the appearance of bedrooms has changed considerably in the last few years and they have evolved into a diaphanous, open atmosphere, affording an ideal place for rest. In this case, the simpleness of lines is one of the predominate notes, thus attaining ambiences where the flow of light through space is essential. Therefore, designers are searching for a simplification of shapes and volumes that are able to transmit, at the same time, a sensation of comfort and well-being.

The most important companies of contemporary design usually offer furniture designs that integrate the bed, the wardrobe, and the bureau or complements, thus achieving perfect harmony of materials and colors. Regarding the beds, usually they are at floor level, which is inspired from the traditional Japanese aesthetics, but they are also adapted to the western canons of comfort. Natural materials, like wood for the bedstead and the head, or, in the case of upholstered models, cotton, linen or leather, are the most commonly used owing to their capacity to bring warmth to the atmosphere. One of the latest tendencies is to design a very large head of the bed which may extend up to the ceiling or to the sides and thus become original night tables or even shelves which become integrated into the structure of the bed.

In regards to the wardrobes, they have incorporated materials which until only a few years ago were not perceived as appropriate for this type of furniture.Now used are materials such as aluminum, glass, plastic or methacrylate, with smooth surfaces that reflect this search for the essential and the desire to avoid overloading the space. The new modular systems allow you to design personalized distributions which adapt to the needs of each individual.

*Club 8 Company* Proposal.

The interior of a wardrobe from the "Varia" Program by *Poliform*.

Bed from the "Double" Series by
Piero Lissoni. *Matteograssi.*

Bedroom from the "Apta" Program
by Antonio Citterio. *Maxalto.*

"Grandlit" by Hans Sandgren Jakobsen.
*Fredericia Furniture.*

"Lys" bed by Marco Acerbis.
*Acerbis International.*

"Mo" by Philipp Mainzer. *e15.*

"Raft" Model. *Innovation.*

Proposal by *Club 8 Company.*

"Pei" Model. *Innovation.*

Proposal by *Club 8 Company.*

Closet from the "Apta" Program
by Antonio Citterio. *Maxalto.*

Composition from the "Le Notti" Collection
by Claudio Silvestrin. *Mobileffe.*

Detail of the Dressing Table from the "Le Notti"
Collection by Claudio Silvestrin. *Mobileffe.*

"Pio" Bed by Chi Wing Lo. *Giorgetti.*

Composition from the "Culture"
Collection by Giulio Dalto. *Rattan Wood.*

"Grace" Bed designed and
produced by *Kelly Hoppen*.

Composition from the "Plan" Collection.
*Matteograssi.*

Bedroom from the "Pi" Program.
*Juventa.*

Composition from the "Openside" Program
by Franco Poli. *Matteograssi.*

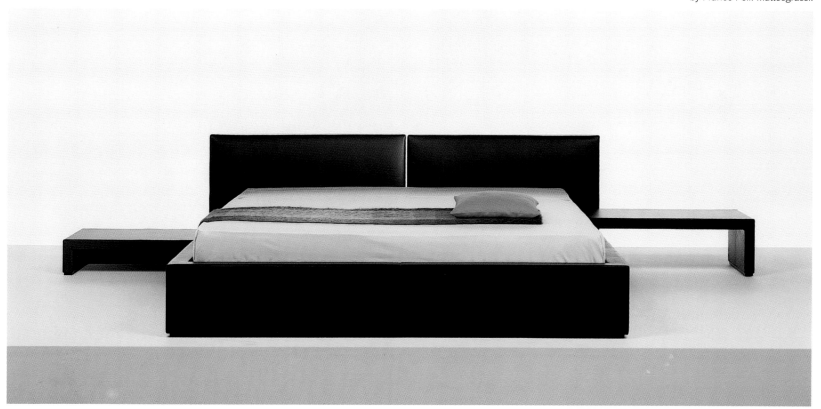

107

"Sleepy Working Bed" by Philippe Starck.
*Cassina* (photo Miro Zagnoli).

Dresser from the "Plan" Program.
*Misura Emme.*

Closet from the "Apta" Program by Antonio Citterio. *Maxalto.*

Proposal from the *Porro* firm.

"Click" Table Lamp by
Ramón Isern. *Vibia.*

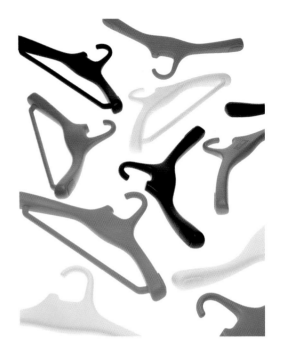

"Hercules" Hangers by Marc Newson.
*Magis.*

Wardrobe with wheels proposed
by the firm *Fredericia Furniture.*

"Zen" Model. *Innovation.*

"Wheel" Model. *Innovation.*

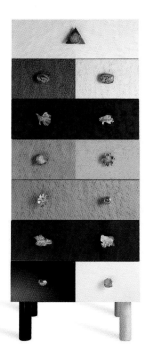

"Genesio" Bureau by A. Cavaliere. *Zanotta.*

"Calamobio" Bureau by Alessandro Mendini. *Zanotta.*

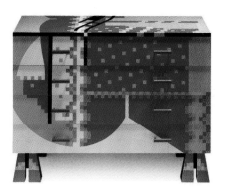

"Marlo" Model by Afra and
Tobia Scarpa. *Molteni & C.*

Wardrobe from the "Sistema Midi"
by Francesc Rifé. *Mobles mb.*

Wardrobe proposed
by the firm *Maisa*.

"Noor" Bedroom by Lodovico Acerbis.
*Acerbis International.*

"Invisible" Bed by I. Bride.
*Zanotta.*

Wardrobe from the "Ki" Program.
*Misura Emme.*

Wardrobe from the "Armadio"
Program. *Misura Emme.*

Bed from the "Ross" Series
by Ennio Arosio. *Mobileffe.*

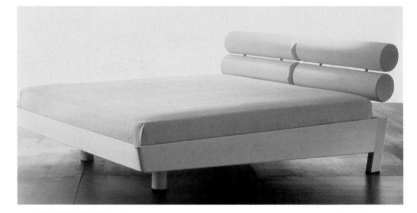

Different proposals from the "Bes" Model
by Massimo Scolani. *Giorgetti.*

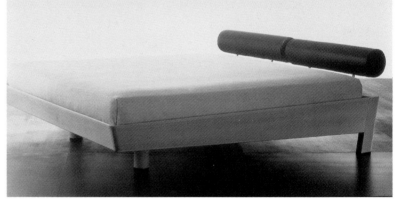

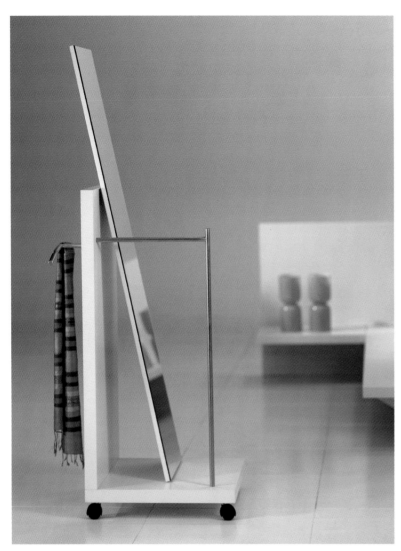

Mirror from the "Pi" Program. *Juventa.*

"Skin" Mirror by A. Quaggiotto,
Pio and Tito Toso. *Cattelan Italy.*

Ceiling Light from the "Ilde" Series
by David Abad. *Dab.*

"Serafi" Closet with wheels.
*Yamakado.*

Bed from the "Apta" Program
by Antonio Citterio. *Maxalto.*

Wardrobe from the "Rex" Program.
*Misura Emme.*

Composition from the "TM Line"
Collection. *Domus.*

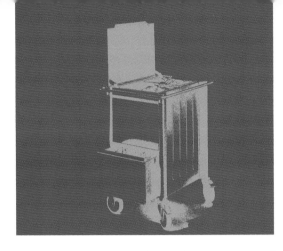

# KITCHENS

In the design of kitchens the focus is mainly on attaining maximum ergonomy and functionality. Being one of the most lived in and used spaces in the household where food is prepared, cooked, stored and eaten, the furniture and layout must optimize the available space, apart from affording the users the maximum comfort and freedom of movements.

Therefore, research and technological innovation have a special importance in these atmospheres as they manage to improve the usability of the different elements with designs that adapt to the specific needs of each home. Materials that are not easily dirtied and guarantee perfect impermeability; modular storage furniture that can be situated at the most convenient height depending on the user while at the same time adapting to the available space; drawers which can be completely taken out thus increasing their available storage space; cupboards with sliding or folding doors which allow for greater mobility; flexibility of diverse modules and complements; rationalization of the interior distribution of storage furniture that allows the maximum and ideal organization of kitchen utensils and food; the stacking of appliances which increases significantly their ease of use; these are some of the latest innovations that have made their way into kitchens, thus facilitating to a great extent the chores in the area with the most life and activity in the home.

In regards to aesthetics, in the last few years designs inspired from industrial design predominate so you can find aluminum or steel surfaces which are combined with wood or glass, or with lacquered doors with bright colors which give a dynamic and juvenile appearance, and where special emphasis is placed on details and the finishing touches.

Stools designed by the firm *Vibiemme*.

"Nuvola" Kitchen by
Luca Meda. *Dada*.

Water area which combines stone
and wood, by *Minotti Cucine.*

The sink and the wall covering are integrated
in this proposal by *Minotti Cucine.*

The stone of the covering is extended thus forming a table or work surface. *Minotti Cucine.*

"Sonica" Chair by Arkiline and "Cube" Table. *Calligaris.*

"Basic" Composition from the
Emporium line. *Schiffini.*

Composition from the "Banco"
Program by Luca Meda. *Dada.*

Composition from the "Nuvola" Program
by Luca Meda. *Dada.*

"Quadrante" Program
by Ferrucio Laviani. *Dada.*

"Flo" Fold-up Ladder by
Marcello Ziliani. *Magis.*

"Tuttifrutti" Storage Cart by
Stefano Giovannoni. *Magis.*

"Gibus" Plastic Bins by
Klaus Hackl. *Magis*.

"Yu Yu" Stools by Stefano
Giovannoni. *Magis*.

"Stand By" Stackable Containers by Axel Kufus
and Studio Tecnico from the firm *Magis*.

Detail from the "Evergreen" Model
by Zengiaro Associati. *Febal.*

Modular Kitchen Furniture from
"Sistema 20". *Bulthaup.*

"Centra" Suspension Lamp
by David Abad. *Dab.*

Modular Shelves from the "Seatlle"
System by Enzo Mari. *Robots.*

"Viso" Jug by Alessandro Mendini. *Alessi.*

Oil Cruet designed by Michael Graves. *Alessi.*

Jugs designed by Mario Botta. *Alessi.*

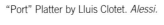

"Port" Platter by Lluis Clotet. *Alessi.*

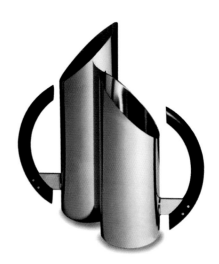

"Tea for Two" Tea Set by
Achille Castiglioni. *Alessi.*

Electric Water Heater designed
by Michael Graves. *Alessi.*

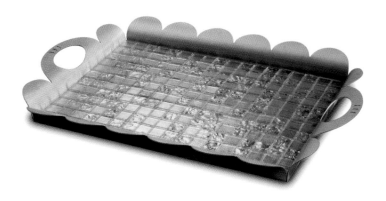

"Recinto Luna" Tray by
Alessandro Mendini. *Alessi.*

"Piccolo Recinto" Tray, "Anna Sugar" Sugar Bowl and "Anna
Creamer" Creamer by A. Mendini and A. Margarini. *Alessi.*

131

Composition from the "Banco"
Program by Luca Meda. *Dada.*

Composition from the "Vela"
Program by Luca Meda. *Dada.*

Compostion with the dining room integrated, designed by *Bulthaup.*

Composition from the "Flipper"
Model by Zengiaro Associati. *Febal.*

"Chef" Lighting System for the Kitchen
by Proli Diffusion Studio. *Vibia.*

"Favia" Suspension Lamp
by Proli Diffusion Studio. *Vibia.*

"Verdi" Stool by *Habitat.*

"Cosmos" Ceiling Light for the Kitchen by Ramón Isern. *Vibia*.

"Tempi Duri" Wall Clock by Marcello Ziliani. Produce *Progetti*.

Composition from the "Vega" Model
by Silvano Barsacchi. *Scavolini.*

"Perla" Program, a creation
from the firm *Lube Over.*

Compostion from the "Sally M.I."
Program by Phoem. *Febal.*

Possible Combination from the "Lime"
Model by Zengiaro Associati. *Febal.*

One of the possible compositions from the
"Banko" Program by Enrico Tonucci. *Triangolo.*

The diverse modules from the "Sistema 25"
can be combined in numerous ways. *Bulthaup.*

Picture from the "Lemon" Model by
Zengiaro Associati. *Febal.*

Composition of great elegance from the
"Sistema 25" by *Bulthaup.*

Detail of the range area from the "Vela"
Program by Luca Meda. *Dada*.

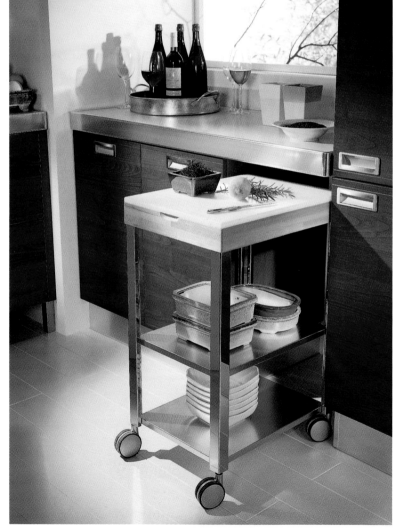

Detail of the pull-out cart from the "Melville"
Program by Silvano Barsacchi. *Scavolini*.

Composition of the "Sistema 20"
Program. *Bulthaup.*

Picture of the detail of the pull-out Spice Box from
the "Sistema 25". Bulthaup.

Table and Drawers Set from the
"Sistema 20". *Bulthaup.*

Bin for waste recycling from the
"Sistema 20". *Bulthaup.*

Storage model from the "Sistema 20".
*Bulthaup.*

Module from the "Sistema 20" that has the water area. *Bulthaup.*

Module from the "Sistema 20" that has the cooking area. *Bulthaup.*

Possible combination from the "Lime"
Program by Zengiaro Associati. *Febal.*

Possible combination from the "Banco"
Program by Luca Meda. *Dada.*

Modular composition based on the color white. *Minotti Cucine.*

Wood and natural stone are in perfect harmony in this proposal by *Minotti Cucine.*

# BATHROOMS

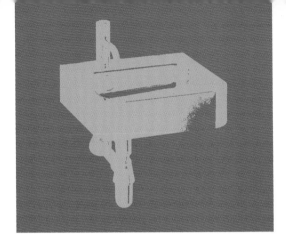

Bathrooms are no longer that dark, boring and impersonal room where very little effort was made to decorate it in a nice way since generally it was outfitted with very basic bathroom fixtures and furniture. Now, they have become a reflection of a new style of life. A new bathroom culture has emerged that has situated the bathroom as one of the main rooms of the home, where water as a regenerating element, has become the principal protagonist. Some of the most well-known designers at the moment are using their talent to do research on new materials and shapes in order to develop a differ-

ent concept of bathroom fixtures, faucets or complementary items. This has resulted in the bathroom becoming the new scenario for creativity and innovation.

The traditional, elliptical-shaped, porcelain washbasin can now be found in numerous new materials such as stainless steel, glass, natural stone and other newer materials such as Duralmond. In respect to the shape, conventions are being broken as you can now find them square, or to the other extreme, completely round. Thus, they are able to personalize these ambiences.

It is common to find in the market complete furniture program designs that allow for multiple combinations which offer very balanced, aesthetic results apart from affording practical and elegant solutions for storage. Normally you can find that the different storage modules are suspended in the air, either supported on legs or fixed to the wall, which gives the composition an air of lightness and weightlessness.

Color, vitality, comfort, quality, and, in short, imagination, fill the bathrooms of the future with articles that give off technical and formal perfection which forever banishes the ordinary routine from these spaces.

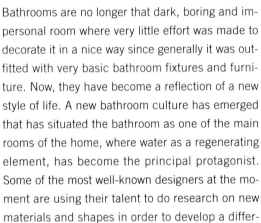

"Waterpot" and Soap Dispenser Faucet by Marcello Ziliani and Gabrielle Pezzini. Made by *Krover.*

"Big" stainless steel Washbasin.
*Industrias Cosmic.*

"Solitude" Bath Column which integrates the washbasin and the shower. *Dornbracht*.

"Roll" Toilet Paper Holder with a reserve by Marcello Ziliani. Made by *Krover*.

"Image" Floor Mirror with a towel bar
by Prospero Rasulo. *Glas.*

"Bipop" Bathroom Closet by Cozza
and Mascheroni. *Desalto.*

149

"Container" Bathroom Furniture
by Xavier Claramunt. *Industrias Cosmic.*

Stainless steel Accessories
by *Vieler International.*

"Gotta" gres porcelain Counter with a glass washbasin. *Altro*.

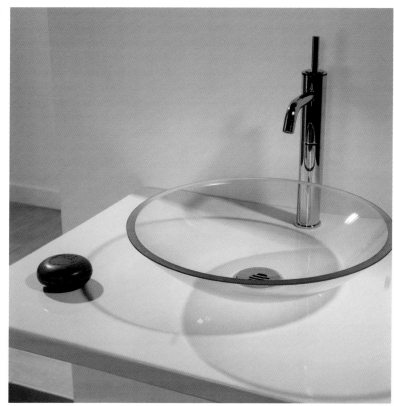

"Dreamscape" Bathroom Series by Michael Graves.
*Dornbracht* (taps); *Duravit* (furniture); *Hoesch* (bathtub).

"Gran Qubik" Set with a ceramic washbasin and a birch wood counter. *Altro.*

Set-in Bathtub with a translucent front.
*Bis Bis Imports Boston.*

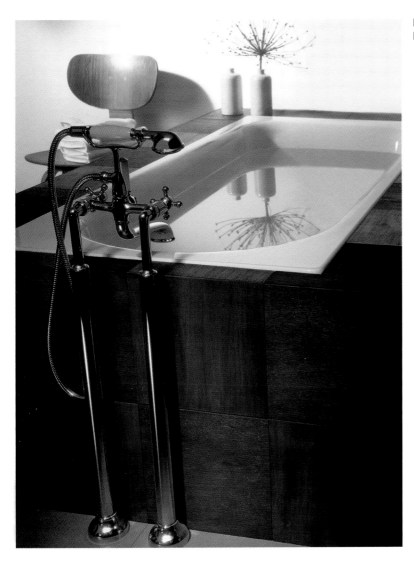

Faucets for the "Madison" Bathtub. *Dornbracht.*

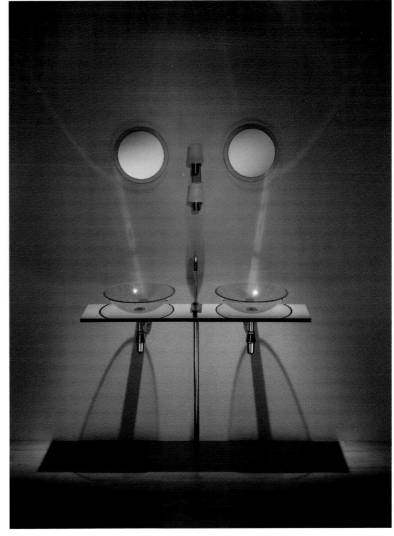

Proposal for the "Top System" Program of custom-designed supports and counters. *Altro.*

"Nomadi" multi-functional Carts
by Giuseppe Canavese. *Methodo.*

Different designs from the "Nomadi"
Collection by Giuseppe Canavese. *Methodo.*

Stainless steel bathroom Complements
from *Vieler International.*

Furniture for the bathroom designed
and produced by *Keramag.*

Washbasin from the "Barcelona"
Series by Matteo Thun. *Rapsel.*

Another model from the "Barcelona"
Collection by Matteo Thun. *Rapsel.*

Faucets for the washbasin designed by Arne Jacobsen. *Vola.*

"Gotta" Counter and "Bol" stainless steel washbasin. *Altro.*

Bathroom furniture from the "System" Program
by Ricard Ferrer. *Industrias Cosmic.*

"Pendolo" Complements for the bathroom
by Marcello Ziliani. Made by *Bertocci.*

Composition from the "Metropolis"
Program by Carlesi Mauro. *Toscoquattro.*

Composition from the "Pluvia" Program
with a marble counter. *Toscoquattro.*

"Carezza Lake" Bathtub by P. Büchele and
"Cobra" Shower by A. Hazebroek. *Rapsel.*

"Quadrotto" Washbasin by
Bruna Rapisarda. *Regia.*

Composition proposed
by the firm *Elledue*.

"Ninfo" Washbasins by Ramón Úbeda,
made of Duralmond. *Rapsel*.

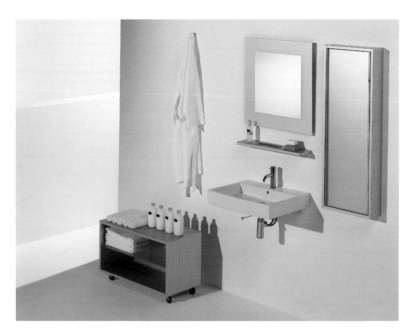

"New Look" Mirror by Cosmic Studio.
*Industrias Cosmic.*

"Lavasca" Bathtub by Matteo Thun,
made of Duralmond. *Rapsel.*

Composition from the "Vivano"
Program. *Keramag*.

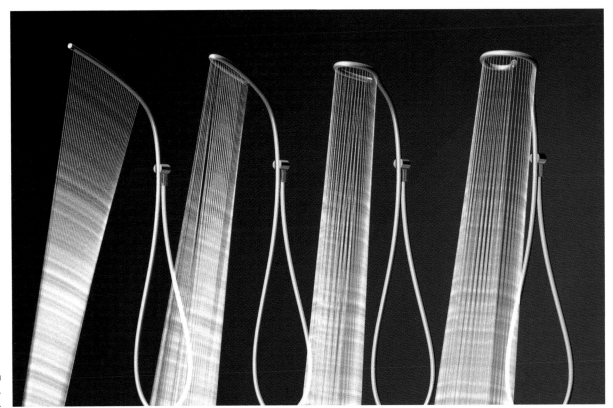

"Sir Biss" Shower Hose with a
modulable nozzle by Marcello Ziliani.
*Wonderful World*.

"Tara" Shower Taps by Sieger Design.
*Dornbracht.*

"Tara" Washbasin Taps by Sieger Design.
*Dornbracht.*

"Visit" courtesy Bathroom. *Keramag.*

Composition from the "Versilia" Series
by Carlesi Mauro. *Toscoquattro.*

165

Detail from the "Feng-Shui" Program by E. Bolis, M. Nespoli and A. Novara. *Toscoquattro.*

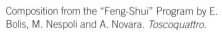

Composition from the "Feng-Shui" Program by E. Bolis, M. Nespoli and A. Novara. *Toscoquattro.*

Composition from the "Zen" Program with a natural stone washbasin. *Toscoquattro.*

Detail from the "Feng-Shui" Program by E. Bolis, M. Nespoli and A. Novara. *Toscoquattro.*

"3002" Composition with stainless
steel washbasins. *Axia*.

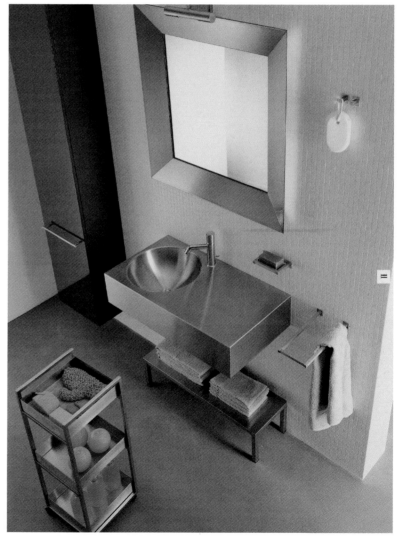

"3003" Composition with a washbasin and
counter made from only one piece of steel. *Axia*.

"3001" Composition where porcelain, wood and steel are combined. *Axia.*

"3006" Composition with a porcelain washbasin. *Axia.*

"Tube" stainless steel Washbasin with a transparent, methacrylate support. *Altro.*

"Kaokaban" or "AQ7" Washbasin
by Toni Arola. *Artquitect Edition.*

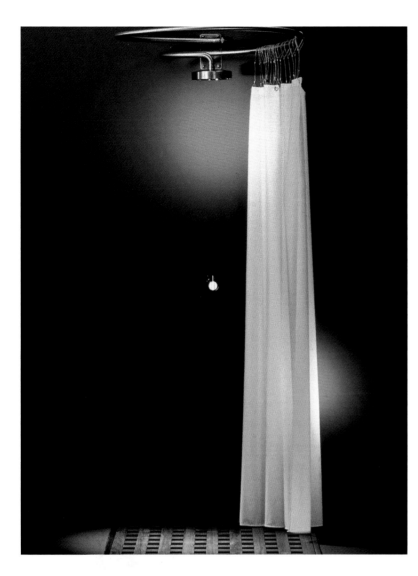

"Pluvia" Shower by Matteo Thun.
*Rapsel.*

"Vero" Washbasin designed
and made by *Duravit.*

# DIRECTORY

ACERBIS International spa
Via Brusaporto 31
24068 Seriate (Bg), ITALY
Tel.  39 0352 94222
Fax. 39 0352 91454
info@acerbisinternational.com

ADELTA
Friedrich-Ebert-Straße 96
46535 Dinslaken, GERMANY
Tel.  49 2064 40797
Fax. 49 2064 40798
adelta@t-online.de

ADRENALINA
C.P.99
47841 Cattolica (Rimini), ITALY
Tel.  39 0721 208372
Fax. 39 0721 209923
adrenalina@adrenalina.it

ALESSI spa
28882 Crusinallo (VB), ITALY
Tel.  39 0323 868611
Fax. 39 0323 641709
comunic.alessi@alessi.com

ALNO AG
88629 Pfullendorf, GERMANY
Tel.  49 07552 21-0
Fax. 49 07552 21 37 89
mail@alno.de

ALTRO
La Coma 18, A1, Pl. Pla de Santa Anna
08272 Sant Fruitós del Bages, SPAIN
Tel.  34 902 104 108
Fax. 34 902 104 109
altro@altro.es

ARTEK
Eteläesplanadi, 18
00139 Helsinki, FINLAND
Tel.  358 9 613 250
Fax. 358 9 6132 5260
info@artek.fi

ARTELANO
57 Rue de Bourgogne
75007 Paris, FRANCE
Tel.  33 1 44420161
Fax. 33 1 44420160
artelano@aol.com

ARTEMIDE
Lérida, 68-70
08820 El Prat de Llobregat (BCN), SPAIN
Tel.  34 934 783 911
Fax. 34 933 707 306
artemide@ict.ictnet.es

ARTQUITECT
Showroom: C/Comercio, 31
08003 Barcelona, SPAIN
Tel.  34 932 683 096
Fax. 34 932 687 773
artquitect@artquitect.net

AXIA srl
Via delle Querce 9
31033 Castelfranco Veneto (Treviso),
ITALY
Tel.  39 0423496222
Fax. 39 042374 3733
axia@axiabath.it

B&B ITALIA spa
Strada Provinciale 32
22060 Novedrate (Como), ITALY
Tel.  39 03179 5213
Fax. 39 03179 5224
beb@bebitalia.it

Bd EDICIONES DE DISEÑO
C/ Mallorca 291
08037 Barcelona, SPAIN
Tel.  34 934 586 909
Fax. 34 932 073 679
bd@bdbarcelona.com

BIS BIS IMPORTS BOSTON
4 Park Plaza
2116 Boston, UNITED ESTATES
Tel.  1 617 350 7565
Fax. 1 617 482 2339
info@bisbis.com

BODEMA
Via Padova 12
20030 Camnago di Lentate sul Seveso,
ITALY
Tel.  39 0362 5572 55-60
Fax. 39 0362 5572 71
bodema@bodema.it

BONALDO spa
Via Straelle 3
35010 Villanova (Padova), ITALY
Tel.  39 049929 9011
Fax. 39 049929 9000
bonaldo@bonaldo.it

BULTHAUP GmbH
84153 Aich, GERMANY
Tel.  49 8741 800
Fax.  49 8741 80 340
www.bulthaup.com

CALLIGARIS
Viale Trieste, 12
33044 Manzano (Udine), ITALY
Tel.  39 04327 48211
Fax.  39 0432 50104
info@calligaris.it

CARPYEN
Pere IV, 78-84
08005 Barcelona, SPAIN
Tel.  34 933 209 990
Fax.  34 933 209 991
comercial@carpyen.com

CASAMILANO
Via Edison 18
20036 Meda (Mi), ITALY
Tel.  39 036234 0499
Fax.  39 036234 1126
info@casamilanohome.com

CASSINA SpA
Via L.Busnelli 1
20036 Meda (Mi), ITALY
Tel.  39 03623 721
Fax.  39 03623 422 46
info@cassina.it

CATTELAN ITALIA Spa
Via Pilastri 15 z.i. Ovest
36010 Carre' (Vi), ITALY
Tel.  39 0445 318711
Fax.  390445314289
info@cattelanitalia.com

CLASSICON
Perchtinger Strasse 8
81379 München, GERMANY
Tel.  49 089 748133-0
Fax.  49 089 7809996
info@classicon.com

CLUB 8 COMPANY
Fabriksvej, 4 -P.O. Box 74
6870 Ogold, DENMARK
Tel.  45 7013 1366
Fax.  45 7013 1367
club8@club8.com

COR SITZMÖBEL
Nonenstraße 12
D-33378 Rheda-Wiedenbrück,
GERMANY
Tel.  49 0 5242 4102-0
info@cor.de

DADA
Strada Provinciale 31
20010 Mesero, ITALY
Tel.  39 02 9720791
Fax.  39 02 97289561
dada@dadaweb.it

DESALTO
Via per Montesolaro
22063 Cantú (Como), ITALY
Tel.  39 0 31 700 481
Fax.  39 0 31 700 112
oma@desalto.it

DIEMO ALFONS
Rosenthaler Straße 19
10119 Berlín, GERMANY
Tel.  49 3085 22975
Fax.  49 3085 964353

DAB-DISEÑO ACTUAL BARCELONA
Avda. de la Cerdanya, Nau 10; Pol. Ind.
Pomar de Dalt
08915 Badalona (Barcelona), SPAIN
Tel.  34 934 650 818
Fax.  34 934 654 635
info@dab.es

DO+CE MUEBLES DOCE,S.L.
Pol.Ind.Massanassa C/N.1 Nave 44
46470 Massanassa (Valencia), SPAIN
Tel.  34 961 252 467
Fax.  34 961 252 554
doce@do-ce.com

DOMUS CENTRAL
Crta. Nacional 332, nº 23, Km 88
03550 San Juan (Alicante), SPAIN
Tel.  34 965 943 360
Fax.  34 965 943 361
domus@domuscentral.com

DORNBRACHT
Köbbingser Mühle, 6
58640 Iserlohn, GERMANY
Tel.  49 0 2371 433 0
Fax.  49 0 2371 433 232
mail@dornbracht.de

DURAVIT ESPAÑA
Balmes 184, 4º 1ª
08006 Barcelona, SPAIN
Tel.  34 932 386 020
Fax.  34 932 386 023
info@es.duravit.com

E15 GMBH
Hospitalstraße 4
61440 Oberursel, GERMANY
Tel.  49 6171 5 82577
Fax.  49  6171 582578
asche@e15.com

EDRA spa
Via Livornese Est 106
56030 Perignano (Pisa), ITALY
Tel.  39 058761 6660
Fax.  39 058761 7500

ELLEDUE ARREDOBAGNO-GRUPO
COPAT
Viale L. Zanussi, 9
33070 Maron di Brugnera (Pn)
ITALY
Tel.  39 0434 617111
Fax.  39 0434 617212
info@copat.it

FEBAL CUCINE
Via Provinciale 11
61025 Montelabbate, ITALY
Tel.  39 0721 426262
Fax.  39 0721 426284
export@febal.it

FIAM ITALIA spa
Via Ancona 1/b
61010 Tavullia (Pesaro), ITALY
Tel.  39 07212 0051
Fax.  39 072120 2432
fiam@fiamitalia.it

FONTANA ARTE spa
Alzaia Trieste, 49
20094 Corsico (Milano), ITALY
Tel.  39 0245121
Fax.  39 024512660
info@fontanaarte.it

FREDERICIA FURNITURE
Treldevej 183
7000 Fredericia, DENMARK
Tel.  45 75 92 3344
Fax.  45 75 92 3876
sales@fredericia.com

GALLOTTI & RADICE
Via Matteoti 17
22072 Cermenate, ITALY
Tel.  39 031 77 7111
Fax.  39 031 77 7188

GANDIA BLASCO
Musico Vert, 4
46870 Onteniente (Valencia), SPAIN
Tel.  34 962 911 320
Fax.  34 962 913 044
gandiablasco@gandiablasco.com

GIORGETTI spa
Via Manzoni 20
20036 Meda (Mi), ITALY
Tel.  39 03627 5275
Fax.  39 03627 5575
giorspa@giorgetti-spa.it

GIOVANETTI srl
Via Perucciani 2
51034 Casalguidi (Pistola), ITALY
Tel.  39 057394 6222
Fax.  39 057394 6224
giovannetti@ftbcc.it

GLAS
Via Cavour 29
20050 Macherio (Mi), ITALY
Tel.  39 039232 3202
Fax.  39 039232 3212
glas@glasitalia.com

GRUPPO INDUSTRIALE BUSNELLI
Via Kennedy, 34
20020 Misinto (MI), ITALY
Tel.  39 02 96320221
Fax.  39 02 96329384
gruppo@busnelli.it

HABITAT
Pº de la Castellana 79
28046 Madrid, SPAIN
Tel. 915 553 354

HABITAT
Colón 34
46004 Valencia, SPAIN
Tel.  963 944 112

HABITAT
Diagonal 514
08006 Barcelona, SPAIN
Tel.  934 154 455

HABITAT
C.C. El Triangle; Pl. Catalunya, 4
Barcelona, SPAIN
Tel.   933 017 484

INDUSTRIAS COSMIC
C/ Cerdanya, 2-Pol. Ind. La Borda-
Apdo.Correos 184
08140 Caldes de Montbui (Barcelona),
SPAIN
Tel.   34 938 654 277
Fax.  34 938 654 264
cosmic@icosmic.com

INGO MAURER GmbH
Kaiserstrasse 47
80801 München, GERMANY
Tel.   49 089 381 6060
Fax.  49 089 381 60620
www.ingo-maurer.com

INNOVATION RANDERS
Blommevej 38
8900 Randers, DENMARK
Tel.   45 86 43 8211
Fax.  45 86 43 8488
mail@inno.dk

INSA srl
Localita' Canova 1
27017 Pieve Porto Morone (Pavia), ITALY
Tel.   39 038272 7411
Fax.  39 038278 8111
info@insa.it

ISOKON PLUS
Turnham Green Terrace Mews
W41QU Chiswick (London),
UNITED KINGDOM
Tel.   44 020 89940636
Fax.  44 020 89945635
ply@isokonplus.com

JUVENTA
Slipstraat, 4
8880 Ledegem, BELGIUM
Tel.   32 56 50 01 91
Fax.  32 56 50 39 37
juventa@juventa.be

KAGAN NEW YORK COLLECTION
P.O. BOX 286434
NY 10128 Nueva York, USA
Tel.   212 289 0031
Fax.  212 360 7307
info@vladimirkagan.com

KELLY HOPPEN INTERIORS
2 Munden Street
W14 0RH Londres, UNITED KINGDOM
Tel.   44 020 7471 3350
Fax.  44 020 7471 3351
www.kellyhoppen.com

KERAMAG AG
Kreuzerkamp 11
D-40878 Ratingen, GERMANY
Tel.   49 (0) 2102/916-0
Fax.  49 (0) 2102/916-245
info@keramag.de

KLENK WOHN COLLECTIONEN
Industriestraße 34
72221 Haiterbach, GERMANY
Tel.   49 7456 93820
Fax.  49 7456 938240
klenk-collection@t-online.de

LAGO srl
Via Morosini 22/24
35010 San Giogio in Bosco (Padova),
ITALY
Tel.   39 049599 4299
Fax.  39 049599 4199
info@lago.it

LAMBERT GMBH
Konstantinstraße 303
41238 Mönchengladbach, GERMANY
Tel.   49 2166 86830
Fax.  49 2166 859638
office@lambert-home.de

LEOLUX
Kazernestraat 15
5928 Venlo, HOLLAND
Tel.   31 77 3 87 72 16
Fax.  31 77 3 87 72 88
lba@leolux.nl

LUBE OVER CUCINE
Dell'Industria 4
62010 Treia, ITALY
Tel.   39 07 33 84 01
Fax.  39 07 33 84 01 15
www.lubeover.it

LUZIFER
Pie de la Cruz, 5-19
46001 Valencia, SPAIN
Tel.   34 963 912 124
Fax.  34 963 913 431
www.luziferlamps.com

MAGIS
Via Magnadola 15
31045 Motta di Livenza (Treviso),
ITALY
Tel.   39 04 22 76 87 42-3
Fax.  39 04 22 76 63 95
magisuno@tin.it

MAISA sas di Sergio Meroni & C.
Corso Garibaldi  80
20020 Seveso (Mi), ITALY
Tel.   39 036250 0971
Fax.  39 036250 0974

MARCELLO ZILIANI
Via Amba d'Oro 68
25123 Brescia, ITALY
Tel.   39 030 363758
Fax.  39 030 360430
mz@marcelloziliani.com

MATTEO GRASSI
Via Padre Rovanati, 2
22066 Mariano Comense, ITALY
Tel.   39 031 757 711
Fax.  39 031 748 388
info@matteograssi.it

MAXALTO
Strada Provinciale 32
22060 Novedrate (Como), ITALY
Tel.   39 03179 5213
Fax.  39 03179 5224
beb@bebitalia.it

mb - MOBLES BELLMUNT
C. del Puig, 12
08050 Roda de Ter  (Barcelona),
SPAIN
Tel.   93 850 00 38
Fax.  93 850 02 45
moblesbellmunt@infonegocio.com

METHODO srl
Via Molinetto, 70
31030 Saletto di Breda di Piave (TV),
ITALY
Tel.   39 0422 686132
Fax.  39 0422 686587
info@methodotp.com

MINOTTI CUCINE
Via Napoleone, 31
37015 Ponton (Vr), ITALY
Tel.   39 045 6860464
Fax.  39 045 7732678
info@minotticucine.it

MISCEL·LÀNIA DE MERCÈ BOHIGAS
Pl. del Sol, 3-4, 1-2
08950 Esplugues de Llobregat,
SPAIN
Tel.   34 934 731 133
Fax.  34 934 732 600
miscelania@miscelania.com

MISURA EMME
Via IV Novembre, 72
22066 Mariano Comense(Co), ITALY
Tel.   39 031 754111
Fax.  39 031 754111
info@misuraemme.it

MOBILEFFE spa
Via Ozanam, 4
20031 Cesano Maderno (Mi), ITALY
Tel.   39 03625 2941
Fax.  39 036250 2212
info@mobileffe.com

MOLTENI & C. Spa
Via Rossini 50
20034 Giussano (Mi), ITALY
Tel.   39 0362 3591
Fax.  39 036285 2337
www.molteni.it

MONTANA MØBLER
Akkerupvej 16
5683 Haarby, DENMARK
Tel.   45 64 73 32 111
Fax.  45 64 73 32 38
montana@montana.dk

MONTIS
Steenstraat 2-postbus 153
5100 AD Dongen, HOLLAND
Tel.   31 (0) 162 377777
Fax.  31 (0) 162 377711
info@montis.nl

NANI MARQUINA
Carrer  Església 4-6, 3er D
08024 Barcelona, SPAIN
Tel.   932 376 465
Fax.  932 175 774
info@nanimarquina.com

PEROBELL
Avda. Arraona 23
08205 Sabadell (Barcelona), SPAIN
Tel.   34 937 457 900
Fax.  34 937 271 500
info@perobell.com

POLIFORM spa
Via Monte Santo 28
22044 Inverigo (Como), ITALY
Tel.  39 031 6951
Fax. 39 03169 9444
info.poliform@poliform.it

PORRO INDUSTRIA MOBILI srl
Via per Cantu' 35
22060 Montesolaro (Como), ITALY
Tel.  39 03178 0237
Fax. 39 03178 1529
info@porro.com

RAFEMAR
Apdo. Correos 98
08240 Manresa, SPAIN
Tel.  34 938 784 810
Fax.34 938 745 014
rafemar@rafemar.com

RAPSEL
Via Volta 13
20019 Settimo Milanese (Milano),
ITALIA
Tel. 39 02 33 55 981
www.rapsel.it

RATTAN WOOD spa
Via S.Rocco 37
31010 Moriago (Treviso), ITALIA
Tel. 39 043896 6307
Fax. 39 043896 6413
info@rattanwood.it

REGIA
Via Vigevano, Zona Industriale
20053 Taccona di Muggiò (MI), ITALIA
Tel. 39 039 2782510
Fax. 39 039 2782571
info@regia.it

ROBOTS SPA
Via Galvani 7
20082 Binasco (Milano), ITALIA
Tel. 39 02 90 54 661
Fax. 39 02 90 54 664
info@robots.it

ROLF BENZ AG &Co.KG
Haiterbacher Strasse 104
72202 Nagold , ALEMANIA
Tel. 49 7452 601245
Fax. 49 7452 601110
sroemer@rolf-benz.de

ROSENTHAL AG
Wittelsbacherstrasse 43
95100 Selb, GERMANY
Tel. 49 0 9287/72-0
Fax. 49 0 9287/72-271
www.rosenthal.de

ROSSI DI ALBIZZATE
Via Mazzini, 1; Casella postale n°59
21041 Albizzate (Varese), ITALY
Tel. 39 0331 993200
Fax. 39 0331 991583
info@rossidialbizzate.it

SANTA & COLE
Stma. Trinidad del Monte, 10
08017 Barcelona, SPAIN
Tel. 34 934 183 396
Fax. 34 934 183 812
info@santacole.com

SCAVOLINI SPA
Via Risara 60-70/ 74-78
61025 Montelabbate, ITALY
Tel.  39 07 21 44 31
Fax. 39 07 21 44 34 04
contact@scavolini.com

SCHIFFINI MOBILI CUCINE
Via Genova 206
19020 Ceparana, ITALY
Tel. 39 01 87 95 01
Fax. 39 01 87 93 23 99
schiffini@luna.it

STOKKE
Apdo. Correos 181; Av. Vizcaya 67
20800 Zarautz, SPAIN
Tel. 34 943 130 596
Fax. 34 943 133 201
stokke_spain@redestb.es

STUA
Poligono 26
20115 Astigarraga, SPAIN
Tel. 34 943 330 188
Fax. 34 943 556 002
stua@stua.com

STYLING S.R.L. (GRUPO BONALDO)
Via dell' Industria, 2
35010 Borgoricco, ITALY
Tel. 39 49 9318711
Fax. 39 49 9318700
styling@styling.it

TECTA
Sohnreystraße 10
37697 Lauenförde, GERMANY
Tel. 49 5273 37890
Fax. 49 5273 378933
info@tecta.de

THONET, GEBRÜDER
Michael Thonet Straße 1
35066 Frankenberg, GERMANY
Tel. 49 6451 5080
Fax. 49 6451 508108
info@thonet.de

TISETTANTA Spa
Via Tofane, 37
20034 Giussano (Mi), ITALY
Tel.  39 0362 3191
www.tisettanta.it

TOBIAS GRAU
Siemensstrasse 35 B
D-25462 Rellingen, GERMANY
Tel. 49 4101 3700
Fax. 49 4101 3701000
info@tobias-grau.com

TONELLI Srl
Via della Produzione 33-49
61025 Montelabbate, ITALY
Tel. 39 07 2148 1172
Fax. 39 07 2148 1291
tonelli@tonellidesign.com

TOSCOQUATTRO srl
Via Sila, 40 c
59100 Prato, ITALIA
Tel.  39 0574 815535
Fax. 39 0574 815384
toscoquattro@toscoquattro.it

TRIANGOLO S.R.L.
Via Icaro 10
61100 Pesaro, ITALY
Tel.  39 07 21 42 53
Fax. 39 07 21 42 53 25
triangolo@triangolo.com

VIBIA
Barcelona, 72-74
08820 El Prat de Llobregat (BCN),
SPAIN
Tel. 34 934 796 970
Fax: 34 934 796 973
www.vibia.es

VIBIEMME srl
Via Cividale 44
33044 Manzano (Udine), ITALY
Tel. 39 043275 0473
Fax. 39 043274 0050
vibiemme@vibiemme.it

VICCARBE
Travesia Camí del racó, s/n
46469 Beniparrell (Valencia), SPAIN
Tel. 34 961 201 010
Fax. 34 961 211 211
viccarbe@viccarbe.com

VIELER INTERNATIONAL
Breslauer Straße 34
D-58614 Iserlohn, GERMANY
Tel.  49 02374/52-0
Fax. 49 02374 52268
info@vieler.com

VITRA INTERNATIONAL AG
Klünenfeldstrasse 22
CH-4127 Birsfelden, SWITZERLAND
Tel.  4161 3770000
Fax. 4161 3771510
www.vitra.com

VITRA HISPANA S.A.
Pza. Marqués de Salamanca 10, 1°
dcha.
28006 Madrid, SPAIN
Tel.  34 914 264 560
Fax. 34 915 783 217
www.vitra.com

VOLA A/S
Lunavej 2
DK-8700 Horsens, DENMARK
Tel.  45 7023 5500
Fax. 45 7023 5511
sales@vela.dk

YAMAKADO
Viaduc des Arts- 65, Avenue Daumesnil
75012 París, FRANCE
Tel.  33 0 1 43 407979
Fax. 33 0 1 43 407980
yamakad@aol.com

ZANOTTA spa
Via Vittorio Veneto 57
20054 Nova Milanese (Mi), ITALY
Tel.  39 0362 4981
Fax. 39 036245 1038
zanottaspa@zanotta.it